The Business Traveling Parent
How to Stay Close to Your Kids When You're Far Away

By Dan Verdick
Illustrated by Scott Pollack

Robins Lane Press
a division of Gryphon House, Inc.

Beltsville, MD
www.robinslane.com

For Elizabeth and Olivia

The Business Traveling Parent

How to Stay Close to Your Kids When You're Far Away

Over 100 Ideas, Tips, & Hints for Before You Leave, While You're Gone, and When You Return

Dan Verdick

Illustrated by Scott Pollack

Robins Lane Press
a division of Gryphon House, Inc.
Beltsville, MD

Copyright © 2000 Dan Verdick

Published by Robins Lane Press, A Division of Gryphon House, Inc., 10726 Tucker Street, Beltsville MD 20705

Visit us on the web at www.robinslane.com

Cover and Text Illustration by: Scott Pollack

Libary of Congress Cataloging-in-Publication Data

Verdick, Dan, 1965
   The business traveling parent: how to stay close to your kids when you're far away / by Dan Verdick.

      p. cm.
   Includes index.
   ISBN 0-87659-211-6
   1. Games for travelers. 2. Business travel. 3. Travelers—Family relationships. I. Title.

GV1206 V47 2000
649'.51—dc21

                                                    00-022948

Table of Contents

Before You Go Activities

While You're Away 45

In-A-Hurry Activities

While You're Away Activities

When You Come Home 79

In-A-Hurry Activities

When You Come Home Activities

Introduction

"He took his first step today, honey!" "Mom, I scored the winning basket!" "Dad, I wish you were here to help me with my homework." "When are you coming home?"

Family life is filled with little milestones, and for a business traveling parent, this means it's likely that your child will do something momentous while you're in another city, sitting alone waiting for room service, or calling from a pay phone at an airport. Add to this the fact that younger children don't always understand why you have to go away—or how long it will be until you're home—and you've got even more reasons for stress and anxiety than the usual trials and tribulations of traveling.

We're all familiar with the joys of being away on business—the layovers, delays, materials not arriving, mistakes in reservations, lost luggage, and the pressures of the big presentation or meeting. But for business traveling parents, it also means having to spend precious time away from loved ones.

The goal of this book is simple: to help you, as a parent, make the most of your situation. Business travel may take you away from your family more than you would like, but it also gives you a unique chance to play games and do activities with your children. You have the chance to have fun and learn with your children in special ways. These games and activities will make the time away seem shorter and the time together more enjoyable.

How to Use This Book

The Business Traveling Parent is designed to be extremely easy to use. Each of the three parts of the book starts with general advice, followed by "In-a-Hurry" activities, because chances are you have very little time on your hands when you're a business traveler.

Following these quick ideas are more in-depth activities that you can do when you have a little more time before an upcoming trip. "Variations" follow some of these activities to give you ideas for making them more age-appropriate for your child. "Follow-up" follows some of these activities, offering ideas on how to expand the activity into other aspects of your child's life. Throughout the book are quotes from real business traveling parents, who share how they balance demanding work schedules and family and offer tips on how to make business trips easier on the whole family.

All of the activities—whether "In-a-Hurry" or more involved—can be tailored to work with your family and life. Use the imagination and creativity of each family member. You can even use business travel as a way to begin family traditions that will provide cherished memories.

Finally, remember to keep your child involved in your life and stay involved in his. Even if business travel seems routine to you, it has aspects that your kids might find fascinating. In their eyes, you get to ride on airplanes, jump into taxis, and visit exotic places. With just a little time and effort, the idea of traveling on business and being away from the kids will seem less like a difficult fact of life and more like the chance to discover, grow, and have lots of fun!

A few things to keep in mind:

• One of the easiest things to do is often the most overlooked: Talk to your child about your business trip. Explain where you're going and why. Pull out a map or globe and find your destination together. Tell your child where you'll stay, what you'll do, and who else might be going along on the trip. Be sure to say how much you'll miss her while you're gone. Most of all, listen to what she has to say about your trip, and what you can do together.

• Focus on process, not product. The activity doesn't need to be perfect—you just want to have fun together.

• Choose activities that fit your child's age level and interests. If one activity doesn't work, do another one. Add your own variations. Return to familiar activities you love.

• Remember the Milestone Rule: It doesn't count until you see it. In other words, if you miss one of your child's firsts—a lost tooth, a piano recital, or a home run—don't dwell on the fact that you weren't there to see it happen. There will be other opportunities to view these first-hand, so make a big deal of them then, too. This way your child gets to celebrate "firsts" twice!

• Don't forget the needs of your spouse when you're trying to juggle work and family. If your spouse is the one who travels, it might be fun to always pack a little surprise in his or her suitcase (kids often love being part of a surprise activity). Leave a loving note beneath clothes, tuck in a special edible treat, or have your child write or draw a "Miss You" note and hide it in the luggage.

Last but not least, it's always tempting to bring home presents after each trip, but this can get expensive! You don't have to spend a fortune to give your child something special. Collect postcards from the hotel gift shop, bring home the travel-size toiletries from your hotel, or pick up some inexpensive souvenirs. Encourage your child to keep a scrapbook or collection of items from your trips. And above all, remember: Bringing yourself home after a long business trip is the best present of all.

Before You Go

In-A-Hurry Activities

Before You Go Activities

Before You Go

There are basically two types of business trips: the one that's been on your calendar for weeks and the one that sneaks up on you suddenly. With either one, getting ready often feels like a hassle. You have to arrange and confirm travel plans or put your schedule in the hands of an agent or assistant. You may need to rush to complete work for the trip, pack, fight traffic and get to the airport or station, land, get to the place you're staying, check messages, return e-mails, send faxes, make phone calls, and more. On top of all that, you need to make sure that your work at the office will be covered while you're away.

But what may be the most difficult is the schedule-juggling that takes place at home as a result of your trip. You may have to make special arrangements for childcare and babysitters, and it's up to your spouse and children to take care of all the household duties alone. Your spouse and children may also have to juggle their schedules to accommodate your impending trip. Your child may not even understand why you have to leave. These added issues often increase the guilt you feel about leaving your family.

Remember, even if you don't have much time before you go, you can still do some little things that will mean a lot to your child. This section will provide you with some ideas and activities for softening the blow of your upcoming absence. From simply spending time together before you go to scheduling when you'll send her mail, you and your child will find one or more of these activities helpful in creating long-distance bonds.

The kids always know that when I'm going on a trip they can stick something in my suitcase as a surprise. Sometimes it's something really sweet, like a picture of Mommy with them, or sometimes it's funny, like a rubber snake my reptile-loving son put in a dress shoe. I don't know what it will be until I unpack. It's my favorite part of my first night away.

–Cynthia, a direct marketing professional and the mother of Anthony, four, and Jennifer, two

Did You Get My Note?

Write a "love note" to your child, saying how much you'll miss him or her while you're away. Put it someplace where your child is sure to see it after you're gone: on a bed pillow, taped to the bathroom mirror, hidden inside a sock drawer. For an unexpected twist, tuck the note in a surprise place where it may not be found right away: in your child's backpack, on the dashboard of the car, or even in the refrigerator.

Variation

Ask your child to write you a note or draw a picture. After you leave the room, have your child hide it in your luggage. (Your spouse can help younger children with this activity, because they may also remove items you need for your trip!)

Where Are You Going?

Using a map or atlas, tracing paper, and a pencil, trace the outline of your destination (state, country, or province). Then draw a large dot on the city or town where you'll stay, and for older kids, mark other nearby areas. Challenge your kids to fill in the missing names of the places you've traced and marked. See if they can find and name the capital of the region or other well-known locations.

Variation

Have them page through the atlas or go to the map to see where the drawing "fits."

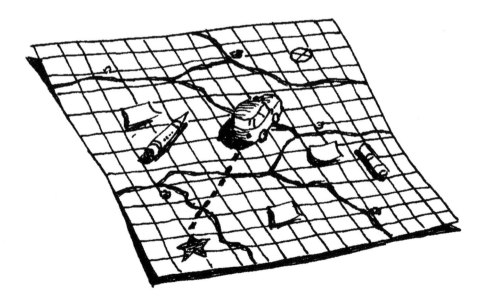

Itinerary Swap

Give your child copies of your flight itinerary, daily agenda, and any other materials that detail your trip schedule. Ask him or her to create his or her own detailed itinerary for the time you're gone, showing what he or she will be doing during and after school and on weekends. This way, both you and your young "assistant" will know exactly where the other will be during the days you're gone.

Before You Go Tip

Reading maps is a great way to help your children learn about geography and travel, and locating your destination helps them see exactly where you'll be. Keep a variety of maps handy and pull them out before you travel.

IN-A-HURRY ACTIVITIES

It's For You!

Review your travel schedule and your children's schedules; decide together the best times for you (or them) to call. Mark these times on both schedules. Have your children use stickers or draw a telephone on the calendar. You may want to schedule these calls as near as you can to big events, so it's easier for you to share in the moment. Even if schedules are tight, a little time on the phone can mean the world to younger children. For older kids, it's a great way to have a conversation and stay in touch despite busy schedules.

Before You Go Tip

Collect travel-related items such as maps, coloring books with a travel theme, stickers of airplanes, and so on, depending on your child's age and interests. Pull these out for your child before each trip. When you return, put these items away for the next trip. This way they'll be viewed as special items to look forward to enjoying. Don't forget to restock!

Family Checklist

Together, brainstorm a list of things that need to be done around the house before you go. Include anything that comes to mind, both the necessary and the silly, from giving the dog a bath to making little beds for a collection of stuffed animals. Then, with your kids' help, prioritize the list, and get started on the chores as a group.

> *Breakfast on Mondays is always a special event. Since I don't cook, my wife always makes a special meal for all of us. We talk about the week, and I make sure everyone has a chance to say what they're going to do, including the youngest, who comes up with all sorts of activities for my time away. We all confirm when I'll be calling during the week. Then I drive to the airport, and I'm off to my job.*
>
> —Patrick, a health care professional, has three children, ages three to five. He commutes from the East Coast to his job in the Midwest every week.

A Farewell Meal

This is one of the easiest ways to establish a routine around your business travel. Make something special out of your last dinner or breakfast before you leave. If you're pressed for time, have a pizza delivered or order take-out. If you have more time, you can be the chef. Have fun and enjoy a meal together.

Create a Keepsake Box

Together with your children, decorate a folder, binder, or even a large shoebox for them to store any art or schoolwork while you're out of town. Then, when you return, you can make an event of going through the box and talking about the contents. Did someone do well on a test? Or make a special art project? Did anybody learn something fun at school? Encourage your children to include any items they choose— paintings, writings, or even a pressed flower or leaf.

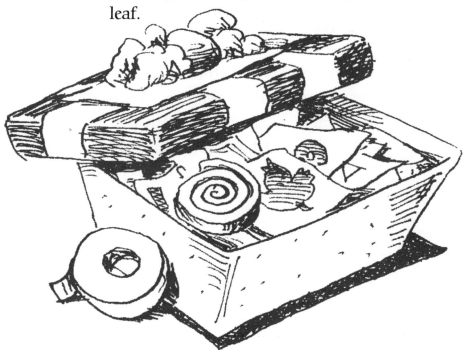

Reschedule a Big Day

Before You Go Tip

If older kids may be alone more while you're away, remind them of the "house rules" before you go— keep the door locked, don't let any strangers in the house no matter what, and other safety rules. Ask them to come up with their own ideas to keep safe until Mom or Dad comes home. Post reminders of safety tips on the refrigerator, as well as information on how to reach you in case of an emergency.

You may not be able to be home for every important day, but you can reschedule a celebration for when you're back in town. It's best to talk to kids honestly—you will be gone for their birthday, but with rescheduling, it will be like having two birthdays this year! Mark the calendar with the real birthday and the day you'll celebrate together. Make a point of calling on the actual day of the event to remind your child of the second celebration to come.

Make a Travel Journal

With just a stapler, two pieces of construction paper, and some notebook paper, you can create a homemade travel journal together. Make the front and back covers from the construction paper, and use the notebook paper for the interior pages. Staple the journal together and ask your kids to decorate it for you. Start a collection of travel journals for your child, one for each trip you take. Record your thoughts in the journal while you're away. Include collections of items that interest them—like postcards of famous buildings or animals as well as writings to them that they can enjoy even years later.

Added Responsibility

Things still need to be done around the house while you're away, so get your child involved. Even toddlers can do some chores, and all kids feel a little more grown up and independent when they complete certain tasks on their own. Together make a to-do list of daily jobs that need to be done—anything from feeding the fish to cooking a meal, depending on your child's age level. Let your child know how important it is to help out every day, but especially while one parent is away.

Mail Call

For your upcoming trip, make a mail schedule for each child, specifying which day is "theirs" to go to the mailbox. During your trip, send notes, letters, cards, and even packages from your destination. Your kids will enjoy sorting the mail and finding which goodies are for them.

Note

To avoid any disappointment related to mail delays, leave a few prewritten notes with your spouse—something as simple as "Love you and miss you" or "Thinking of you." Your spouse can call these special deliveries.

Start a New Book Together

Your leaving for a business trip is a wonderful reason to begin a tradition of starting a new book with your child the night before you go. Visit the library or bookstore together and choose a book that looks fun and easy to update over the phone. You can easily tailor this activity to encourage a love of books in very young children ("We get to read a *new* bedtime story the night before Mom travels!"), or to explore more advanced reading for older kids, who will want to share plot details and retell the story when you're on the phone or when you return. And when you're gone, children can be reminded each time they read the story that you'll be home soon to share it with them again.

Surfing Time

If you have a computer at home, search the Internet for information about your destination with your child before you go. What famous sites are there to see? What kinds of plants and animals live there? What does the hotel look like? Are there any famous buildings? What other things can you find out about where you're going?

Before You Go Tip

Stock up on stamps and stationery for you and your children. Paper warehouses and party supply stores are great sources for finding inexpensive writing paper and envelopes. This makes it that much easier to stay in touch.

Special Times Together

Arrange a time with your child to do a favorite activity together before you go. Even a half-hour will seem special if you set the time aside to play your child's favorite card game or take a walk through the woods.

Before You Go Tip

Make the most of your time right up to when you leave. Could you reschedule a flight to depart in the evening so you can spend some time with the kids after school? Could your family start a tradition of having breakfast together if you always take a late-morning flight? Could the whole family take you to the airport and see you off?

BEFORE YOU GO ACTIVITIES

Letters Home

Use stationery you made together ahead of time!

What to Do

For stationery, decorate the paper with your names, drawings of the family, or stickers of airplanes and other travel- or destination-related images. Make sure your child leaves space for you to write the letter.

For mailing labels, write your child's name and address, and decorate the label with crayons or markers. Do similar decorations for the envelopes.

When you go on your business trip, keep the stationery and labels handy for writing a quick letter home. To make it even easier for you to mail homemade letters, let your child put the stamps on the envelopes before you go.

What You'll Need

Writing paper

Markers, pens, crayons, and other writing materials

Sheet of large labels or adhesive-backed paper

Blank envelopes, any size

Stickers (optional)

Variations

Look for paper-making kits at art stores and let your child make the stationery with you. Decorate the paper with glitter, stickers, or rubber stamps.

Follow-up

You may want to emphasize words your child is beginning to learn, or words to look up in a dictionary, in your letters home. Have a storage place where your child can save the letters on "family letterhead" from you.

Treasure Hunt

Leave a trail of "clues" that leads to a treasure!

What to Do

First, pick out a "treasure" for your child. It could be anything—a new book, a toy, or movie tickets. Hide the treasure in a secret place. In another spot, hide a note that hints to where you've hidden the treasure. In yet another spot, hide a note that hints to where the first note is. In this way, work backward to create a "trail" of three or four notes.

What You'll Need

Paper and pen for writing notes

Hidden treasure!

Just before you leave on your trip, stick a note on the bathroom mirror, on your child's pillow, or in another obvious spot that hints to where the first clue can be found. While you're wing- ing your way to your destination, your child will relish going on his or her own custom-made treasure hunt!

Hint

It may be helpful to prepare the "note trail" with your spouse, so he or she can help if your child gets stumped.

Variations

• An older child can draw a map of your house or yard, which he can then use as a map for locating hidden treasure. Leave the treasure map as your last clue with a place marked for your child to find the hidden treasure.

• For an unexpected twist, put all the clues in surprise places where they may not be found right away: in your child's backpack, on the dashboard of the car, or in the refrigerator.

• Have your child lead you on a treasure hunt when you get back, with the first clue taped to the front door.

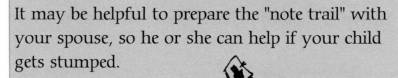

How's the Weather?

Here's a new twist on an old standby—talking about the weather.

What to Do

With your child, cut weather symbols from construction paper. Make yellow suns, blue raindrops, and grey clouds. Ask your child if they can think of others; if he can, cut out a few of those, too.

Ask your child to track the weather for you while you're gone, so you will know what you missed. Every day, he can look outside to see what the weather's like. Then, with the help of your spouse, he can tape the appropriate symbol on that day's square on the calendar.

What You'll Need

Construction paper

Scissors

Tape

Calendar

Growing and Caring

Plant something that will grow while you're gone.

What to Do

What You'll Need

A small plant or seeds

Potting soil

A clay pot or other planter

Gravel

Visit a nursery before you go, and select a plant or seed packet together. Have your child put a layer of gravel in the bottom of a clay pot for drainage, and then add the potting soil. Follow the nursery instructions for transplanting, or plant the seeds to the depth recommended. Have your child water the soil, every day if needed, and take notes about the plant's growth or the seeds' sprouting while you're away.

Variations

You can be creative about all the aspects of indoor and outdoor gardening with your children. Together, custom-paint clay pots or metal watering cans, buy matching gardening gloves, and make your own plant signs that show what varieties you've planted. If you enjoy gardening already, and you do this every time you travel, you may soon have an indoor garden that you made with your child.

Have Suitcase, Will Travel

A fun way to make unique identification tags with your child.

What to Do

What You'll Need

Large labels

Construction paper

Scissors

Markers, pens, or crayons

Colorful yarn

Hole punch

A copy store with a lamination machine

Write or type out your name and address onto large labels decorated by your child. Then cut them to fit on a slightly larger piece of construction paper. Together with your child, cut out shapes of airplanes or suitcases. Apply the address labels to the colorful cutouts. Take them to a copy store and have them laminated. Then, near the top of each tag, punch one hole and attach the tag to your suitcase handle with yarn.

Variations

For a luggage marker you can spot right away, braid some pieces of colorful yarn and tie them around the handle of your luggage. You'll never pick up the wrong bag again.

Before You Go Tip

Ask your child to help you pack, or to simply sit and chat while you do. Younger children will feel like helpers if you assign them to choose your socks, find a certain scarf, or place other items in your suitcase. Older children can give you advice about what to wear, if they want! Let an older child call the taxi to schedule your pick-up (you may want to listen in to make sure it's done right). In these ways, you can turn the "chores" of get-ting ready for business travel into quality time with your child.

You Can Reach Me At This Number

A fun way to leave your phone number for the family!

What You'll Need

Magnets (available at art supply stores)

Construction paper

Scissors

Markers

Glue

What to Do

Make magnetic numbers for the "1", area code, and the numbers where you'll be staying. You can cut out numbers from construction paper and paste magnets on the back, or draw the numbers on with colorful markers to paper you've glued onto small magnets. You can even make additional magnet numbers for the room number you'll have once you check in.

Together, you and your child can spell out the phone number on the fridge. Just make sure you leave the number on paper somewhere handy in case the magnetic numbers get rearranged while you're gone.

Variations

Use this activity for your cellular phone or pager number if you'll be available for a call before you get back to the hotel.

World Wide Web

Keep track of all the places you've gone on business trips and log family vacations, too!

What to Do

What You'll Need

A large map—of the world, or of the continent, country, state, or province where you travel

Colorful yarn

Pushpins or thumbtacks

Scissors

Ruler or measuring tape

On the map, use a pushpin to mark the city or town where you live. Together with your child, find your destination and mark it with another pushpin. Measure how much yarn you'll need to string up (you may even have your child hold one end), cut the yarn to fit, and pin it between the two locations. Use a different color yarn for each trip, and soon you'll have a map covered with a colorful record of your travels.

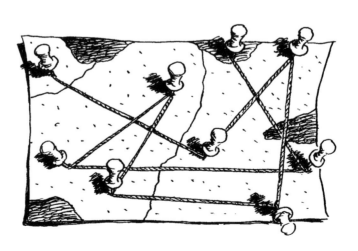

Variations

You can use yarn for flight paths, too, if you have connecting flights, or for older kids, calculate mileage flown by using the mileage key on the map.

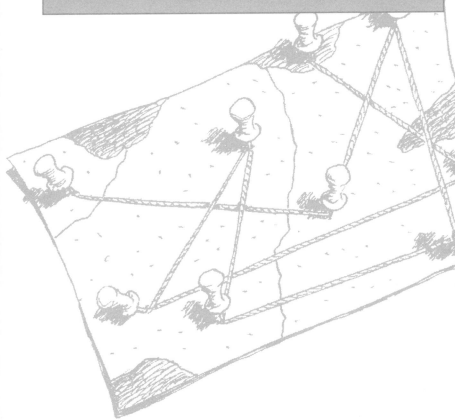

Business Traveling Parent Tip

A large map around the house is a wonderful learning tool and a good way for you and your child to see at a glance where you're traveling. Splurge and devote an entire wall to the largest map you can find, or keep a good children's atlas in a handy place for easy reference.

Mapmaker, Mapmaker, Make Me a Map

Make a map puzzle that your kids can play with again and again.

What to Do

What You'll Need

Map of state, country, or region where you will be traveling

Cardboard

Paste or rubber cement

Carpet knife

Shoebox

Using a carpet knife, trim a piece of cardboard to the same dimensions as your map. Paste or rubber-cement the map to the cardboard. When it dries, cut it into crazy-shaped pieces with the carpet knife.

Piece together the puzzle with your child. As you do, point out cities you are going to or that you have visited; show what routes you may drive.

Store your puzzle in the shoebox, and give it to your child to play with while you're away.

Before You Go Tip

Always be ready for business traveling parent action! Fill your briefcase or travel bag with home-made postcards, your family's kid-made stationery, hand-made mailing labels (for more about how to make these items, see pages 19-20), envelopes, and stamps to make it easy to dash off a note to your child.

Counting the Days

Leaving for a business trip is a great chance to teach numbers and time to your children.

What to Do

What You'll Need

Large calendar

Markers

Construction paper

Scissors

Glue, pushpins, or tape

Make construction paper numerals for the amount of time you'll be gone—for instance, if you will be gone for four days, make the numbers one through four. Help a younger child draw numbers you'll cut out. Together, find the dates of your trip on a large calendar, and paste, tape, or pin the numbers on the calendar to show how many days are left until you come home. On the first day of your trip, paste the four, on the next day, the three, and so on.

Every time your child asks you or your spouse how long it will be until you're home, mention the number line you created together.

Variations

- Decorate the numbers to relate them to where you're going. Make cowboy and cowgirl hats for Texas, or skyscrapers for New York City, for example. Find images in magazines and catalogs that can be cut out and pasted to the calendar for your theme business trip.

- Have your child make smaller numbers for pasting in your personal business calendar–you'll have a colorful reminder each time you check your own schedule on the road.

Business Traveling Parent Tip

With a busy family, chances are you already have a calendar up on a wall somewhere. Make sure it is large enough, or that there is another larger calendar within reach of your children, so they can have fun with their own dates and schedules as well as those of the business trips you take.

Taxi!

Play taxi driver by making your very own cab!

What to Do

What You'll Need

Large sheets of cardboard (from packing or shipping boxes)

Chairs

Shoebox (with a cardboard flag, this will be your fare meter)

Markers

Glue

Children can learn the word for the funny-looking yellow car at a very young age. Out of large pieces of cardboard, which you can make to stand up by leaning on chairs. Use a black marker to make checkered designs like a taxi. Place the chairs in the middle of the "doors" of the cab. Remember, it doesn't need to look perfect to be fun.

Now, teach your young customer the proper
way to hail a cab (with a yell and an extended
arm, or with a whistle). Let her name the destination (the more outlandish the better), and
when you arrive, pay you with pretend money.
Switch places so she can speed around to get
you to your meeting on time. Have fun making
engine noises and screeching tires as you race
around the city. Step on it!

Variations

You can make your own airplane as easily as a
taxi cab and have fun giving a tour of the sites
outside the little round windows you cut in the
cardboard cabin walls.

Off to the Station

Show your children planes and trains up close.

What to Do

What You'll Need

Time

Most airports and train depots offer tours to the general public. This can be an especially exciting activity for older kids who are beginning to develop hobbies or interests in locomotives or flying machines.

Set up a time well in advance so you can make the most of a family day at the airport or railroad yard. Ask to see if you can have a close look (and feel) of a jet taking off or landing—it can be an incredible experience for a young

child. A tour of the flight control tower and of hangars to look at planes up close can also be part of your visit to the airport.

More to Do

If you travel mostly by air, get books at the library that detail the kinds of jets you fly in, and the history of aviation, railroads, and other modes of transportation. I know one young girl who can tell what type of jet is in the sky if she sees it flying low enough.

Encourage your child's interest by finding reading materials on the science of flight and locomotion, and the heroes and heroines of travel invention. Read with them to learn together how all the machines you ride on a business trip work!

Before You Go Tip

Keep a large calendar in your kitchen or family room to mark with your trips and other events. This way everyone can see when you'll be away and when you'll return. (For more about how to make these items, see pages 34-35.)

You Can Get There From Here

Draw funny pictures of yourself in transit.

What to Do

What You'll Need

Markers, crayons, paint, or other art materials

Paper

Ask your child to think of as many ways as possible that you could get to where you're going. Encourage the fantastic—a dragon or unicorn; the futuristic—a rocket ship or space cruiser; and the humorous—on the back of a turtle or underwater on a whale. Write down each idea that comes up, and paint or draw your business trip "vehicles." Be sure they include a picture of you talking on your cell phone while riding on the dragon's back or with your briefcase on the rocket ship.

For the Birds

A bird feeder is great fun for your child, whether you're at home or on the road.

What to Do

Hang a bird feeder outside in a place where your child can see it easily through a window. Make talking about the feeder a part of your routine while you are home. Every day, ask your child what birds he or she has seen, what colors they were, and how much they ate. Ask if they fought or played, or if they flew alone or in a group. You don't have to be able to identify genus and species to have a good time!

The day before you leave, restock the feeder with food—you can even add extra treats, like fresh orange halves or peanut butter, to attract different birds.

While you are gone, ask your child about the birds at the feeder. What have you missed? Have new birds come to feed? What do they look like?

What You'll Need

A bird feeder

Bird food

Orange halves or peanut butter

Binoculars, if needed

Variation

For more fun, find books that explain how to make your own bird feeders (such as peanut butter balls encrusted with birdseed); these can be especially fun "messes" to make together.

Feeding the Fish

Set up meaningful and fun daily routines for your child before you go.

What to Do

Start your aquarium according to the directions, leaving enough time for the water to reach the right temperature before you go. Visit your local pet store and select a fish or two that are hardy and won't mind (or eat) future aquarium residents. To avoid overcrowding, get items for decorating the aquarium after you've added a few living things.

You can make a household rule that you only add to the aquarium *before* a business trip—this makes it an extra special event. Be sure to schedule enough time to do so before you leave.

This is a very good activity if you know how much you'll be traveling over a year, because your goal will be to add a fish or two before each trip. Fish are pretty simple to take care of, but make sure your child is ready for the responsibility first. Do some research on what kind of aquarium you'll need for your fish.

What You'll Need

Aquarium and supplies (instructions for setting up an aquarium are available at your local pet store)

Fish or other aquarium creatures

This Coupon Is Good For...

Make a special "coupon" good for a date with you when you return.

What to Do

What You'll Need

Construction paper or writing paper

Scissors

Markers, crayons, or pens

Before you leave on your business trip, ask your child to name an activity he would really like to do with you when you get back. Using paper and markers, make a coupon that can be redeemed for that activity upon your return. Your certificate might include pictures of animals to signify a visit to the zoo, or pictures of a favorite place to eat.

The coupon can be good for the simplest of things as well as for activities that take more time and effort. A coupon is a great little reminder of time you'll soon be spending together.

While You're Away

In-A-Hurry Activities

While You're Away Activities

While You're Away

E ven if you think you're too busy on a business trip, you'd be amazed at how much time you have to stay in touch. The key to making the most of your limited time while you're away is to plan, and the key to planning is remembering how much little things can mean to a child. Children love getting postcards or a letter on hotel stationery sent especially to them. Have an idea of a fun gift or things you want to collect to bring home. The little things mean a lot.

If you did even a few of the activities in the "Before You Go" section, you'll already have some tools to help you keep in touch with your child while you're away. This section will provide you with some ideas and activities to maintain that all-important contact with your child, even over long distances.

Remember that travel may be routine (even drudgery) to you, but for kids left at home, your trips may seem really exciting. I was reminded of this on a recent flight when I was seated next to a young boy who was enthusiastic about flying for the first time. During the preflight instructions, most of the adults paid no attention, but the boy turned to his mom and announced, "Cool! The seats float!"

So look at travel from your child's perspective. After all, it is kind of cool that the seats float.

IN-A-HURRY ACTIVITIES

Things I Did to Help

Children love the chance to be helpers when needed, and their efforts to assist while you are away should be recognized and praised.

With your spouse, your child can keep a list of all the ways he or she helped, including doing new tasks usually done by big kids or little chores done around the house.

> *We all wrote a new set of 'tub rules' for when I'm away on business, since bath time is such a big job alone, especially when I'm away for most of the week. The first one out of the tub gets to pick the CD they'll play, the second one out gets to hold the CD case to look at the artwork, and last one out of the tub gets to pull the drain plug. Everyone helps a little more and remembers the rules while Daddy's away. It establishes a routine that makes it easier to get everyone ready for bed.*
>
> Patrick, a health care professional, commutes from the East Coast to his job in the Midwest every week.

It's the Thought That Counts

You don't have to bring a giant stuffed panda home every time you travel (unless you and your child are collecting giant stuffed pandas, and you can get an extra seat on the plane). For a less expensive gift that will also lead to time together, pick up any materials that you come across on your business trip. Children love items from the adult world, so anything will do: convention giveaways, brightly colored materials from a presentation or meeting, items for putting in a scrapbook or for a mobile, or materials that you can cut up and glue together for a mosaic or collage once you're home.

Coins, Coins, Coins

If you travel around the world, bring home some foreign coins, or use foreign stamps in your correspondence.

If you're traveling within the country, collect your change and keep it in a safe place to take home for your kids to count and place in their piggy banks.

While You're Away Tip

Use technology to help you with your parenting. Your laptop, cell phone, pager, home fax, and palmtop can help you stay in touch with your kids. Teach your children how to use the technology on the other end to help them stay in touch with you.

Collecting

For older children, your travel could be an opportunity to start or to add to a collection. Collections are fun ways for children to learn more about their interests, as well as the value of keeping things in good shape.

Whether they're serious collectors or they just like pictures of buildings on postcards, children will look forward to seeing what you've found while you were away or what you send in the mail.

Plus, this is an easy way for you to find sure-to-please surprises for your return home.

You could even start a "travel collection" that includes items such as flags, money (bills and coins), stamps, figurines, or postcards of famous landmarks.

Encourage Journaling

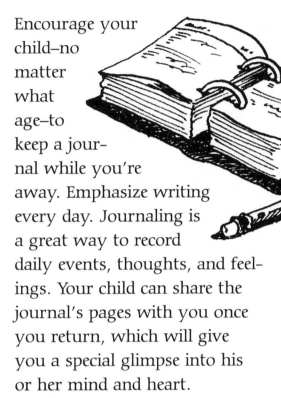

Encourage your child–no matter what age–to keep a journal while you're away. Emphasize writing every day. Journaling is a great way to record daily events, thoughts, and feelings. Your child can share the journal's pages with you once you return, which will give you a special glimpse into his or her mind and heart.

You can keep your own journal on the road as well to show your child that you can write down your own feelings and experiences, too.

While You're Away Tip

Keep a notebook to jot down things you see while traveling that you might want to share with your children. A funny anecdote or a clever exchange between an airline attendant and a passenger make for great stories back home. You'd be surprised how much more observant you become when you carry this type of journal.

Are There Kids Like Me There?

Your child can instantly relate to where you're going if you talk about–and share pictures of–the other children who live there. With a little research, you can find information about places these kids can visit in their hometowns, foods they eat, or things they do for fun.

Even if you're traveling within your own country, you can find information of interest to your child. For example, children in San Diego who get to visit the Pacific Ocean might seem interesting to a child from the landlocked Midwest, and you can bring back pictures of the ocean to share with your child and continue learning about the area you visited.

Be sure to avoid books or pictures that portray demeaning stereotypes. Focus instead on the similarities and differences of children around the world to give your child a fun and enriching learning experience.

Letter on Tape

If you're traveling for an extended time, ask your child to send you a "letter on tape." He or she can speak into a tape recorder, telling you all that's been going on at home and at school. (You'll need to bring a portable cassette player to listen to the tape.) Encourage a creative older child to give a radio news broadcast of the day's events or to write a radio play, complete with an exclusive interview with the family dog, different voices and accents, or homemade sound effects. It can be comforting to hear your child's voice and sense of humor while you're away.

While You're Away Tip

If work or time zones prevent you from reading aloud via phone, tape-record yourself reading a story before you go on your trip. Your child can listen to the tape each night before bed.

While You're Away Tip

Be disciplined about your work schedule. One business traveling parent I know works during the entire flight of his weekly commute—from the moment he sits down in his seat to when it's time to deplane. Making the most of this two hours of work time frees him up in the evening for a phone call or letter home.

Picture This

Take pictures to show or send to your child, so he or she can see what it's like where you are. Have your child take pictures, too, so when you return, she can show you what she did and saw while you were away.

Buy disposable cameras for the two of you, so you won't have to worry about having an expensive camera damaged, lost, or stolen while you're on the road. Ask your child to make a picture book using his or her photos, or make one together after you've had both sets of photos developed.

WHILE YOU'RE AWAY ACTIVITIES

Secret Agent E-mails and Faxes

Create secret codes for writing messages while you're away.

What to Do

Children love creating secret ways to send messages, and a young secret agent can use e-mail, letters, or faxes to get the urgent message to you, the undercover spy.

Quick codes are fairly easy to create, and you may want to have your child make a code for you to decipher, or you can send your own coded message that he or she has to decode. Or agree to a code for a given trip, and send the top-secret communications back to headquarters while you're away.

Here's a simple way to make a code that can be varied in dozens of ways: Write down the alphabet in a straight line on a piece of paper, and then start another alphabet below it, but

What You'll Need

Pen

Paper

Imagination

shifted one letter to the left. For example, *A* would be *B*; *B* would be *C*, etc. For different codes, you can shift the coded alphabet two or any number of letters, or write backward so *A* is *Z*, and *B* is *Y*.

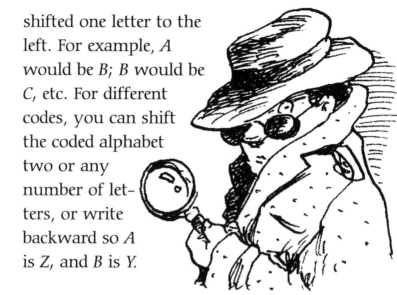

While You're Away Tip

Keep messages very simple for younger kids, like H LHRR XNT UDQX LTBG!, which translates to I MISS YOU VERY MUCH!

Variation

Morse code is another way to write messages and will show kids that codes can be made out of symbols—such as dots and dashes—or that they can draw their own codes for fun. Any number of shapes or symbols can be created for your exchanges.

Follow-up

You can create codebooks for you and your child at home (don't forget a copy for you to take on the road), complete with all the codes you and your child have created together for your business trips. When you travel and send coded messages, be sure to identify which code in the book to use for deciphering each message.

Take Care of Yourself

Take care of yourself while you travel

so you have the energy to keep in touch with your family

and to spend time with them once you get home.

The most disappointing phrase to children of

business traveling parents is, "I'm too tired."

To avoid travel burnout:

Drink plenty of water (air travel is dehydrating).

Get lots of rest.

Get some exercise.

Make use of the hotel gym, or simply
take the stairs or a walk.

Eat right and eat light. You'll feel better during
and after your trip. Restaurants that cater to
business travelers often serve huge portions,
and it can be difficult to resist
the temptation of eating
fast food on the road.

Fun Facts About Where You Are

Gather interesting facts about your location.

What to Do

Ask your child to find some information about the place to help you decide what to see if you have any free time, or encourage his interests by learning fascinating and fun facts about your destination. Together you can research the history, geography, tourist attractions, people, customs, and traditions of the location, as well as anything else that may be interesting for your child to learn. Your child can find materials on states and provinces, as well as the nations of the world, in the school library. On your end, facts about a city or state are easy to

What You'll Need

An encyclopedia, CD-ROM, and other resource books about your destination

Library cards

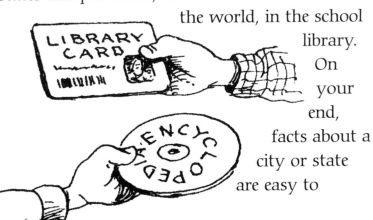

find–they're usually in promotional brochures in your hotel room.

With planning, you can schedule a trip to the public library before you go to give your child a chance to gather information.

Follow-up

Tell your child's teacher or caregiver about the research you're doing together, because it might be a fun opportunity for your child to do even more learning at school.

While You're Away Tip

Don't turn your business travel into a chore or a dreaded time for more homework assignments! The point of doing activities and encouraging learning is for you and your child to stay in touch with each other. Be ready to bend the rules or create whole new variations of an activity.

Where Am I?

Your child guesses where you've gone on business.

What to Do

When you leave on your trip, do not tell your children where you're going. Give them your phone number, fax, or e-mail address; every day, they are allowed to ask three yes-or-no questions. "Is the capital of the state Ames?" "Do they use francs there?" "Does it border an ocean?"

If they guess where you went before you return home, they win. If they're stumped all the way to the airport gate, you win.

What You'll Need

Reference books and related resources

Telephone, fax, and/or e-mail capabilities

WARNING

Be careful, kids are sneaky! One business traveling parent I know "lost" the game to her kids after she had given them the area code and number for faxing questions about where she was. Her kids dialed information and found the city that matched the area code from the operator. She was forced to award them the prize—a free video rental—but the debate still rages on whether that was a fair tactic.

Variation

Award a special prize if your children guess correctly within a day or two of your departure.

While You're Away Tip

Keep information on where you are and where you can be reached in a drawer or tucked away somewhere so it won't interfere with the game but can be easily found by your kids.

Where's the Mystery Spot?

Guess an unknown destination chosen by your child.

What to Do

Before you leave, ask your child to pick a place in the world whose name begins with the same letter as your real destination. Throughout your trip, ask questions of your child via fax, phone, or e-mail. For example: What continent is it on? What is its population? Is it coastal?

What You'll Need

A home travel atlas, globe, or CD-ROM with information about places in the world

Telephone, fax, and/or e-mail capabilities

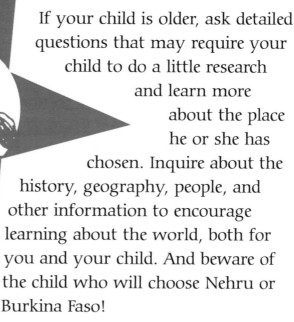

If your child is older, ask detailed questions that may require your child to do a little research and learn more about the place he or she has chosen. Inquire about the history, geography, people, and other information to encourage learning about the world, both for you and your child. And beware of the child who will choose Nehru or Burkina Faso!

Give yourself a chance at a prize, too, as well as a reward for the kids if they stump the business traveler!

While You're Away Tip

Make good use of your traveling "downtime." Those free moments between meetings or during flight delays are perfect for whipping off a quick note to your kids. Downtime is a natural part of travel—learn to use it to keep in touch with your children.

Days of the Week

Your children can create an artistic record of the events you miss.

What to Do

Take several sheets of construction paper and write the days of the week or the days you'll be gone on the top, one day to a page. Let your child write, draw, or paint what happens each day of the week while you're away. Your spouse can help your child draw or look for pictures in magazines or catalogs to tell what happens each day. He or she will be creating a fun log for you to read and admire when you return.

What You'll Need

Construction paper

Markers, crayons, pens, and paint

Scissors

Pictures from magazines or catalogs

Glue

While You're Away Tip

A great way to reduce stress and feel connected to your family is to have reminders of them nearby. For example: Record their voices for prompts on your laptop. Have your child's photo made into a screen saver or mousepad. Bring family photos and artwork made by your kids to display beside your bed or on the mirror. Always carry photos of your loved ones with you in your wallet or briefcase.

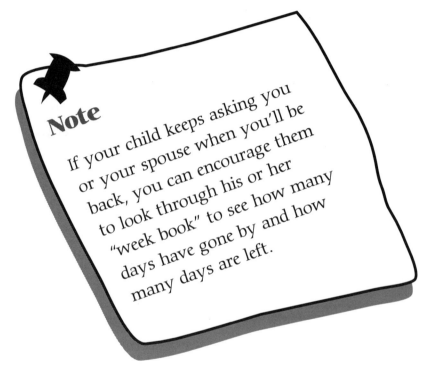

Note

If your child keeps asking you or your spouse when you'll be back, you can encourage them to look through his or her "week book" to see how many days have gone by and how many days are left.

Do You Speak the Language?

Teach your child to write and pronounce foreign words and phrases.

What to Do

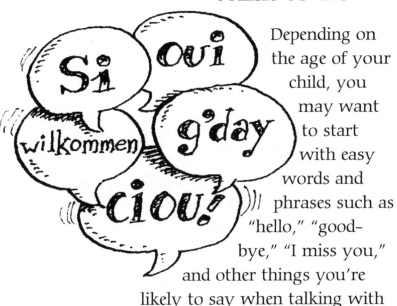

Depending on the age of your child, you may want to start with easy words and phrases such as "hello," "good-bye," "I miss you," and other things you're likely to say when talking with your child on the telephone.

What You'll Need

A language dictionary or CD-ROM good for both children and adults (or use your own knowledge of the language of your destination)

Pens, crayons, and markers

Writing paper

If your child is older, teach him or her some of the phrases you use while doing business.

Variations

Teach your child to spell the words and phrases, so he or she can use them in a letter to you. You can include new phrases in letters home, including some words that your child will have to look up to expand his or her growing vocabulary. And when you talk to your child on the phone, both of you can use the new words you learn together.

Follow-up

Tell your child's teacher or caregiver about your trip, as well as the new words you and your child are working on. The teacher may want to work the words into a lesson or to teach the class a little about the place where you're traveling.

While You're Away Tip

Remember the Milestone Rule: It doesn't count until you see or hear it! "First words at daycare" are not the same as "first words at home" or even "new words for Mom after her business trip."

Secret Telephone Word

Use your hotel's phone number for silly family fun.

What to Do

While you're gone, encourage your child to use the letters associated with the numbers of the telephone keypad to make up a word that corresponds to the digits of the phone number of the place at which you are staying. For instance, 1-800-426-4537 can be "1-800-GANGLES." The more creative and silly the word, the better!

What You'll Need

Writing paper

Pens, crayons, or markers

A telephone

Have a special prize for making the best nonsense word from all of the numbers where you can be reached. Create your own words and definitions—even create your own non-sense-telephone-word diction-ary!

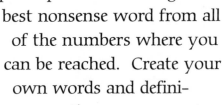

Using the Phone

Using a telephone is an essential skill for your child, especially if he or she will be talking with you regularly on the phone when you're away on business.

Younger children can learn the basics of telephone use, including speaking loudly and clearly.

Older childen can learn about dialing overseas calls, placing collect calls, and using phone etiquette.

Keep phone conversations simple for younger childen, and try to help them understand that they can talk and ask you questions, too.

Write the number where you can be reached in big numerals on a piece of paper, and have your spouse remind your child throughout the day that he or she will be dialing and making a telephone call to you that evening.

When talking with your child, avoid yes or no questions— and elaborate on yes or no questions they ask you. Teenagers can be stubbornly tight-lipped, but showing a genuine interest in their lives, and a willingness to communicate about your own, can be helpful in overcoming that.

Just the Fax

Send fun faxes home to your children.

What to Do

A quick fax can really brighten your children's day, and it only takes a moment of your time. Take a page from a coloring or other activity book, fill out a cover sheet, and fax it home! During your next call home, ask them if they completed the activity, or colored the picture.

What You'll Need

A hotel fax machine

A home fax machine

A coloring or activity book

More to Do

You could take a tip from one business traveling parent I know, who makes a light photocopy of her face to use as her own "fax stationery" that she sends home.   Her young son instantly recognizes them as messages from Mom!

Business Traveling Parent Tip

Reference materials for learning about the world should be available around the house, because your business trip is a great chance to learn together about the places you travel to. These materials will help you and your child gain an understanding of the world and talk about where your trips take you.

Calling for Story Time

Keep bedtime rituals, even when you're away.

What to Do

When you leave home, give your child one copy of the storybook you have chosen. You can surprise them with a new title, or use an old favorite. During your trip, call home every night around bedtime, and read the book with your child over the phone.

Hearing your voice can be comforting just before bedtime, and can reinforce bedtime rituals while you're on the road.

What You'll Need

Two copies of a storybook

Variations

• If your child is learning to read, let her tell the story to you over the phone. This is a great way to practice reading skills!

• Start a tradition of picking up a new book each time you travel.

Encourage the Reading Habit

Remember to encourage reading and literacy at home, both through interacting with your children and by your example. A parent's role in helping children read is a crucial part of childhood development. Whether your children are infants or preteens, make story time a part of getting ready for bed each night–children of all ages benefit from hearing stories told aloud. At home, keep books handy to read together. Let your children see you and your spouse writing letters; reading books, newspapers, and magazines; or sending e-mails and faxes–it will reinforce the importance of reading and the written word.

Travel ABCs

This is a terrific game to play if your child is just learning letters.

What To Do

When you leave, pick a letter from the alphabet. From your departure to your first phone call, your child must come up with as many home-related words as possible that begin with that letter. For your part, you must think of as many travel-related words that begin with that letter. If it helps, you can write them down as you think of them.

During your first phone call home, compare notes. Which of you found the most words? The longest word? The most unusual? Then ask your child to pick another letter, and play another round!

What You'll Need

Imagination

Pen or pencil and paper (optional)

Family Stamps

Give your child a chance at being famous!

What to Do

What You'll Need

Pencils, markers, crayons

Paper

Envelope

Stamps, domestic and foreign

During your international travels, collect stamps from the countries you visit. Once you return, tell your child that the United States Postal Service accepts suggestions for new stamps. (They really do!) Together, design a stamp honoring your child.

When it's done, stick it in an envelope with a letter that includes your return address. Mail it to:

Citizens' Stamp Advisory Committee
c/o Stamp Management, USPS
475 L'Enfant Plaza SW, Room 4474EB
Washington, DC 20260-6756

For more information, go to their website: **http://www.usps.go/websites/depart/stamps**. Who knows? Fame may only be a letter away!

CHAPTER THREE

When You Come Home

In-A-Hurry Activities

When You Come Home Activities

When You Come Home

Now that you're really traveling—and not taking vacation trips or pleasure cruises, but business travel—it's your head that's spinning as well as the world. A 1997 survey of business travelers found that most thought it would take two days to catch up at work as well as two days to catch up at home when they returned from a business trip. Stress and anxiety from business travel can affect you and your

When You Come Home Tip

Share naptime with younger children. If you're completely drained, a nap is a great way to catch up on some of the sleep you lost on your trip. Let your child know that you'll be taking a family nap together. Snuggle and read a book, or be creative about making a nap space— set up camp in front of a movie in the living room, or rest in a shady hammock.

family, and the pressures of traveling may take their toll on you even after you're home. Find a way to reduce your stress. Don't let the anxiety that work is piling up at the office build up inside of you–release it. Exercise, meditation, and simple rest work well. Find a method that works for you and use it. The time you have with your family is too important to be threatened by work-related anxiety.

Travel Journals

If you and your child kept journals during your business travel (see pages 13 and 53 for journaling ideas), read the journals together when you return. Take turns reading each day's entries, and encourage your child's journaling skills. Celebrate new thoughts about his or her feelings, how he or she felt about your being away, his or her accomplishments, and more. Encourage your young writer to listen and comment on your entries, too.

Picnic Lunch

The day you're coming home, ask your family to pack for a picnic, complete with blankets, food and drinks, sunscreen and insect repellent. Keep the food simple and easy to fix, or stop by a take-out restaurant for an easier picnic. When you get home, pick up the kids and head for your favorite park.

Have a fun toy or present from your travels that your child can open and play with outside—bubble makers, Frisbees, or some other fun outdoor item.

Welcome Home!

Nothing will make you feel happier to be home than a "welcome home" sign made by your child for your return (your spouse may have to help with this). Leave your welcome sign up all week.

When You Come Home Tip

Do the things that need to be done around the home as a family. Even younger childen can understand that a lot needs to be done to catch up, especially if they learn that working together is fun and will be followed by playing together. Prioritize what really needs to be done, and let the other things go while you catch up on being mom or dad.

Get Outside

Chances are you've been inside hotels, conference centers, and airplanes on your trip, and you probably haven't had time to get outside and away from the fluorescent lights and reprocessed air of the business world. Coming home from a business trip is the perfect time to "decompress" and get outside with your spouse and child. A walk in a favorite park or a visit to the beach will be a great way to get some fresh air, go barefoot, or swim together. In colder weather, you can take a bike ride or hike.

When You Come Home Tip

Keep your energy up on your last day of traveling. Take a walk after your flight or train ride to rejuvenate. Instead of collapsing on the couch, stretch and take a quick shower when you get home to feel more relaxed and refreshed.

Straight From the Airport

Plan a family out-
ing that starts the
moment after you
arrive, and dress so
you're ready
to go as
soon as you
meet everyone at
the gate. For added
fun, plan a special outing with
your spouse that the kids won't
know about until you arrive,
and drive there from the airport.

When You Come Home Tip

If possible, have everyone come to meet you at the airport or at the gate. Start the reunion as soon as you can, especially if you're flying back on a weekend, when it will be easier for everyone to pick you up.

Adding to Collections

When You Come Home Tip

Take time to talk with your child about your trip, and listen to what he did while you were away. Look at all the artwork and schoolwork that he completed while you were gone.

If you're returning with some items to add to your child's collection or one you work on together, be sure to record where you purchased the item and the date it was added to the collection. This way you'll have a record for more valuable collections, as well as a written history of the collections you're doing for fun.

Cooking Together

When You Come Home Tip

Celebrate your return. Do something special together—order in from your family's favorite restaurant, throw a family party complete with party hats and toasts, or make the night you come home an automatic movie night, complete with popcorn or other snacks.

Cook together on the night you return. Make an Asian meal if you've just come back from Asia, or whip up some salsa if you went to San Antonio. Or just make a meal that's a favorite with your child. Have added fun with your feast by using homemade place mats (see page 97 for details).

Presents Anyone?

When You Come Home Tip

Ask your child to help you unpack so you can all get it out of the way and move on to spending some quality time together (plus you'll feel better having done it right away). Unpacking is a great time to talk, and you can have your child hunt for the presents you stashed in your luggage. Younger children love to be helpers, sorting laundry and putting shoes or clothes away.

If you're like most business traveling parents, your return means that your child may be expecting a present or two (or three). For special presents, anticipation is the key. Make the gift opening wait until after a dinner you've made together or after you've unpacked and had some time to talk together. To make the most of gift giving, hide the surprise in your suitcase and let your child find it while unpacking.

Celebrating Milestones

If your business travel meant that you were away for a birthday, big game, recital, an appearance in a school play, or other milestone event, have the night you come back be "special event" night. Re-celebrate the birthday, or talk about the big game. If your spouse video-taped the event, watch it together. Celebrate the little milestones, too—your child try-ing something new, losing a tooth, or learning more of the alpha-bet.

My, How You've Grown!

When You Come Home Tip

Use your large family calendar as a way to keep the conversation going for a young child who may not remember all the details about what happened each day that you were away. Ask questions based on what your child drew or wrote on the dates you were gone, and be sure to save the decorated months of the calendar as a keepsake.

Use your return from your business trip as a time to measure your child's height, especially if he or she is going through a growth spurt. Measure before you leave so you'll know if any growth has occurred while you were gone. Make a place in your child's room especially for measuring so it's easy to see the height changes over the months and years. And don't just measure height in bare feet and with a perfectly level head—measure how high your child can reach on his or her tiptoes, too.

Time to Adjust

Younger children may need time to adjust

and get used to you again,

and don't be surprised if older kids

initially have emotional reactions you don't expect.

Many business traveling parents say that

upon returning from a trip,

they get a wide range of emotions from their children.

Your child may seem shy, overjoyed, angry, or indifferent.

No matter what the reaction,

respond with extra love and sensitivity.

Remember that this is just

one more reason to maintain emotional connections

with your child each time

you're away on business.

WHEN YOU COME HOME ACTIVITIES

A New Record!

Set speed records for completing chores!

What to Do

The number one rule for this activity is that all jobs (yours as well as your child's) must pass the quality test, whether it's a white glove test for cleaning or inspection of your own sock drawer.

What You'll Need

A stopwatch or clock with second hand

Things that need to be done!

List all the activities you want done, post a reward for record time, and go off to the races. Keep records of your times for each trip; you can see if you are getting any faster at getting the jobs done before the fun rewards are shared by all.

Books in Fun Shapes

Make a fancy travel journal together!

What to Do

Assemble your travel books (one for you, one for your child) with construction paper for the front and back covers and plain paper pages in between. Bind the books together with a stapler. For a different binding, you can punch holes in the book's edge and sew the binding with yarn.

Together, draw what shape you want your travel book to be on the front cover (leaving the book's bound edge intact), and cut along the lines of your drawing. Great shapes for travel books include a round world; an airplane, taxi, or train; or something that reflects what your child did while you were away.

What You'll Need

Construction paper

Plain paper

Hole punch and yarn, or stapler

Scissors

Now use the books to write about what each of you did while you were away, to save the letters you both wrote during your trip, or to store photos and other mementos of your trip.

When You Come Home Tip

Autograph your books! If you and your child sign and date the books you made, you'll create keepsakes of the time you spent together after traveling.

Travel Place Mats

Use your child's art to decorate the dinner table!

What to Do

Together with your child, glue paper artwork and other materials to the construction paper, and color and decorate as you please. You can also add odds and ends from your travel—postcards, stationery, or other paper items you bring home. Write the date of their creation on each one.

When your designs are complete, take them to a copy center that has a laminating machine and have them laminated. They will then be water- and food-proof, and able to be cleaned after use.

What You'll Need

Construction paper

Pens, crayons, and markers

Art by your child

Travel mementos (optional)

A copy store with a lamination machine

More to Do

If you like, you can write other bits of information, too: your child's height, the length of your trip, or a notable achievement your child made while you were gone. In a year or two (or three), these things will be fun to see beneath your dinner plate!

When You Come Home Tip

Leave the technology alone for a while. Turn off the pager, voice mail, e-mail, laptop, and other technologies you have for your work. Catching up on work can wait, at least for a little while.

Mural Painters

Cover your walls with big, fun, parent-child art.

What to Do

On an available floor, lay out newspaper to cre–
ate a work area. On top of the newspaper, roll
out a length of paper that will fit on a wall in
your house. Place books or other heavy objects
on the corners of the paper to keep it flat.

Mark sections of the mural for each day you
were away. In each day's section, paint what
you did that day on the top half, and let your
child paint his or her activities on the bottom
half. Paint pictures of each other talking on the
phone, doing business or schoolwork, and

What You'll Need

Newspapers

A large roll of
paper
(available at party
supply stores or
arts and crafts
stores)

Books or other
heavy objects

Paint, crayons,
markers, and pens

Tape or
thumbtacks

missing or thinking of each other. To simplify this activity for a younger child, draw simple travel- or family-themed pictures.

Give the finished mural a title, sign and date it, and tape or tack it to the wall of your kitchen, family room, or hallway for all to see.

Variations

You can use other materials for a "multimedia" mural—photographs, postcards, letters, or other materials that help you tell the story of what you and your child did to keep in touch.

Time Together

To make the most of your time together at home,
create spaces for special activities around your house.
Create places around the home for reading together,
writing in a journal, doing homework or arts and crafts,
and performing other activities your child enjoys
(like dance, or sports and fitness). This will help
your child concentrate when he or she needs to.
And your child will have materials ready and available
for times when he or she wants to be creative.
For your child's spaces, you'll want to have room
for adults to help and have fun, too. Make sure reading
areas offer a comfortable chair for adults
(with plenty of room for holding a little one),
and that arts and crafts areas have
enough materials to share.

Dance Party

Celebrate your return, get the whole family exercising!

What to Do

What You'll Need

Party decorations—homemade party hats, paper streamers, and other handmade party favors

A cassette player or stereo with music for dancing and having fun

Hold a dance party to welcome yourself home. Decorate the dancing room with streamers and other party decorations, crank the music, and have a great time trying new steps or acting silly.

You can add some fun to the dance party by bringing home musical presents—cassettes or CDs of your child's favorite artists or songs. You can also bring home traditional music from the place you visited.

It's a Grand New Flag

Your child can create a family flag.

What to Do

Before your return home, buy a reproduction of the state or national flag of your location. Once home, you can use this flag as the basis of the family flag you will create.

With your child, draw or paint on a sheet of construction paper the design of your flag. Give yourself a family seal, or put each family member's favorite color in a design. If you or your child are stumped at first, look at the design and symbolism of the flag you brought home for inspiration.

If your child is older, he or she may want to glue or sew fabrics together to make a flag. Hang the finished product above your front door.

What You'll Need

A flag, or a picture of a flag from your destination

Construction paper, markers, pens, and crayons, or colorful fabric scraps

Glue

Hints

Flags make for a great collection! If your child likes them, why not bring one back from every trip? If you can't find the flag you're looking for, America's Best Products (1-800-419-5404) also carries U.S. state flags, as well as many flags from around the world.

Index

A

ABCs, 77
activities. See also games
  aquarium, 43
  before you go, 18
  bird feeder, 41-42
  cooking, 89
  coupons for, 44
  creating spaces for, 101
  dance party, 102
  exercise outdoors, 86
  gardening, 24-25
  handmade journals, 95-96
  luggage tags, 26-27
  making flags, 103-104
  murals, 99-100
  off to the station, 38-39
  picnic lunch, 84
  place mats, 97-98
  reading journals, 83
  and weather, 23
  world wide web, 30-31
adjustment, 93
airplanes, 31, 37
airports, 38-39, 87
America's Best Products, 104
aquariums, 43
art
  making flags, 103-104
  murals, 99-100
  picture drawing, 40
  place mats as, 97-98
  as record, 67-68

B

bird feeders, 41-42
books
  for codes, 59
  to encourage reading, 76
  handmade, 95-96
  and starting new, 16
  and story time, 75
  tape-recording of, 55
boxes, keepsake, 11
burnout, 60

C

calendars
  and conversations, 92
  for family, 39
  and learning numbers, 34-35
  and phone calls, 8
  and rescheduled celebrations, 12
  and weather, 23
cameras, 56
cassette player, 55
celebrations, 12, 89, 91
children, 54
chores
  to encourage responsibility, 14
  list of, before you go, 9
  list of, while you're away, 49
  speed records for, 94
  as when you come home activity, 85

Resources

P. 10 A FAREWELL MEAL

Kids Cooking: A Very Slightly Messy Manual/With Plastic Measuring Spoons
Klutz Press
ISBN 0932592147
$13.95
All ages
Sixty-five kid-friendly recipes to round out any family meal, complete with a set of color-coded measuring spoons.

Honest Pretzels: And 64 Other Amazing Recipes for Cooks Ages 8 & Up
by Mollie Katzen
Tricycle Press
ISBN 1883672880
$19.95
Ages 8 and up
The great thing about cookbooks by Mollie Katzen is that children are the cooks and adults are chef's assistants. All the recipes are vegetarian, very healthy, and employ all sorts of cooking techniques and skills for kids to learn.

Pretend Soup and Other Real Recipes: A Cookbook for Preschoolers & Up
by Mollie Katzen
Tricycle Press
ISBN 1883672066
$16.95
Ages 4-8
A great cookbook for cooking with very young children, this book teaches kids math, science, and working together, all while making things like chocolate-banana shakes and preschool popovers. A classic.

P. 13 MAKE A TRAVEL JOURNAL

All About Me: A Keepsake Journal for Kids
by Linda Kranz
Rising Moon
ISBN 0873586581
$12.95
Ages 9-12
For kids having a tough time getting started and thinking of things to write about, *All About Me* is filled with ideas and starters for the young writer.

Doing the Days: A Year's Worth of Creative Journaling, Drawing, Listening, Reading, Thinking, Arts & Crafts Activities for Children Ages 8-12
by Lorraine M. Dahlstrom
Free Spirit Publishing
ISBN 0915793628
$21.95
Ages 8-12
This book is one year's worth of journal ideas, with hundreds of activities linked to the calendar year.

P. 14 ADDED RESPONSIBILITY

Growing Responsible Kids
By Evelyn Peterson. Illustrated by Barb Tourtillotte
Totline Books
ISBN 1570291020
$9.95
Nearly 100 activities for making responsibility and caring a part of everyday life for your children. Winner of a Parents' Choice Recommended Award.

P. 19 LETTERS HOME

Naomi Wants to Know: Letters from a Little Girl to the Big Big World
by Naomi Shavin
Fairview Press
ISBN 1577490762
$12.95
Ages 6 and up
For aspiring young letter writers, this book is a charming collection of letters that six-year-old Naomi wrote to satisfy her curiosity. She writes Queen Elizabeth II about the Welsh Corgis they have in common, and she writes earthworm scientists to learn more about creepy crawlers. Great ideas for writing together to send letters to the corners of the world.

Papermaking for Kids: Simple Steps to Handcrafted Paper
by Beth Wilkinson. Illustrated by Albert Molnar
Gibbs Smith Publisher
ISBN 0879058277
$10.95
Ages 9-12
For making family stationery, you can use these handcrafted papers for all sorts of fun textures and colors.

P. 23 HOW'S THE WEATHER?

Puddle Jumpers: Fun Weather Projects for Kids
By Jennifer Storey Gillis. Illustrated by Patti Delmonte
Storey Books
ISBN 0882669389
$9.95
Ages 4-8
This book features an assortment of weather projects for fun when it's raining or shining. Check the forecast for when you're gone or for when you return and pick a project to do together.

P. 24 GROWING AND CARING

Garden Crafts for Kids: 50 Great Reasons to Get Your Hands Dirty
by Diane Rhoades
Sterling Publications
ISBN 0806909994
$14.95
All ages
A great how-to book for encouraging the young gardener with an activity for each time you're about to leave on a business trip.

Gardening with Children
by Beth Richardson. Photographs by Lynn Karlin
Taunton Press
ISBN 1561581925
$19.95
All ages
This is a avid gardening book that does a great job of making children a real part of the process, and will help children get interested in all aspects of gardening, from planting to tending.

Windowsill Gardening: Year-Round Indoor Gardening Projects for Kids
Klutz Press
ISBN 1570543666
$4.95
Ages 9-12
Complete instructions for growing fifteen projects on the windowsill any time of the year, this book is perfect for planting right before you go and having exciting results for your young gardener to tell you about over the phone or when you get home.

P. 34 COUNTING THE DAYS

A Child's Calendar
by John Updike. Illustrated by Trina Schart Hyman
Holiday House
ISBN 0823414450
$16.95
Ages 4-8
The famous author and a prize-winning illustrator celebrate the beauty and little things of everyday life—a great introduction to the passing of days and months for younger children.

P. 40 YOU CAN GET THERE FROM HERE

The Kids' World Almanac of Transportation: Rockets, Planes, Trains, Cars, Boats and Other Ways to Get There
by Barbara Stein. Illustrated by John Lane
Pharos Books
ISBN 0886874904
$6.95
Ages 9-12
A fun and instructive guide to how people get there from here, this book includes all means of transport, past, present, and future. Cool stuff about famous cars and boats too, from the Batmobile to the Titanic. Good for even younger readers with help from Mom or Dad.

The Wright Brothers: How They Invented the Airplane
by Russell Freedman, Wilbur Wright, Orville Wright
Holiday House Publishers
ISBN 082341982X
$12.95
Young adult
For young adults interested in airplanes, this is the best book on the story of the Wright Brothers and includes their own

photos and other interesting details of the famous flight at Kitty Hawk. You could make this book part of a field trip to the airport for young aviators-most airports offer tours on a regular schedule and include up close looks at jets and planes.

P. 41 FOR THE BIRDS

Backyard Bird Watching for Kids: How to Attract, Feed, and Provide Homes for Birds
by George H. Harrison and Kit Harrison
Willow Creek Press
ISBN 1572230894
$13.95
Ages 9-12
Includes directions for bird-friendly gardens, feeders, birdhouses, as well as tips for photographing birds and keeping a log of their visits.

Sharing the Wonder of Birds with Kids
by Laura Erickson. Illustrated by Kathryn Marsaa
Pfeifer-Hamilton Publishers
ISBN 1570251290
$14.95
This is a fun-filled guide for making the most of your bird watching together.

P. 51 COINS, COINS, COINS
P. 52 COLLECTING

101 Great Collectibles for Kids
by Diane L. Oswald. Illustrated by Brent Roderick
Antique Trader Books
ISBN 0930625757

$16.95
Ages 9-12
A fun, but informative list of collectibles for kids, this book may mean you'll have to do some looking on your business trip to add to your child's collection. A great starting point for other ideas for starting a collection too.

2000 Standard Catalog of World Coins
by Chester L. Krause and Clifford Mishler
Krause Publications
ISBN 087341750X
$47.95
The best resource book on the coins of the world minted since 1901. Thousands of photos, great for looking at current foreign coins as well as the collectible and valuable coins from countries across the globe.

P. 53 ENCOURAGE JOURNALING

All About Me: A Keepsake Journal for Kids
by Linda Kranz
Rising Moon
ISBN 0873586581
$12.95
Ages 9-12
For kids having a tough time getting started and thinking of things to write about, *All About Me* is filled with ideas and starters for the young writer.

Doing the Days: A Year's Worth of Creative Journaling, Drawing, Listening, Reading, Thinking, Arts & Crafts Activities for Children Ages 8-12
by Lorraine M. Dahlstrom
Free Spirit Publishing
ISBN 0915793628

$21.95
Ages 8-12
This book is one year's worth of journal ideas, with hundreds of activities linked to the calendar year.

P. 61 FUN FACTS ABOUT WHERE YOU ARE

How & Why Stories: World Tales Kids Can Read and Tell
By Mitch Weiss. Illustrated by Carol Lyon
August House Publishers
ISBN 0874835615
$12.95
Ages 4-8
If you're traveling around the globe, these are great stories to share with your child about the legends and folklore from places around the world.

P. 63 WHERE AM I?

How & Why Stories: World Tales Kids Can Read and Tell
By Mitch Weiss. Illustrated by Carol Lyon
August House Publishers
ISBN 0874835615
$12.95
Ages 4-8
If you're traveling around the globe, these are great stories to share with your child about the legends and folklore from places around the world.

The Kids' Book of the 50 Great States: A State-by-State Scrapbook Filled with Facts, Maps, Puzzles, Poems, Photos, and More
Scholastic Trade

ISBN 0590996215
$14.95
Ages 6 and up
Gather ideas for items to bring back to your child based on what's listed in this scrapbook on the U.S. states. There's room for photos you take on your trip and for all sorts of memories and souvenirs.

The Scrambled States of America
by Laurie Keller
Henry Holt & Company
ISBN 0805058028
$16.95
The states of the U.S. get all mixed up in this fun children's story. All of the states are brightly colored shapes for younger readers to learn when you read together.

World Almanac for Kids 2000
Edited by Elaine Israel and World Almanac
St. Martin's Press
ISBN 0886878403
$10.95
Ages 9-12
The ultimate almanac for kids, including regular information like flags, history, and facts, as well as a great updated list of Web sites for further learning. For elementary readers too.

P. 65 WHERE'S THE MYSTERY SPOT?

How & Why Stories: World Tales Kids Can Read and Tell
By Mitch Weiss. Illustrated by Carol Lyon
August House Publishers
ISBN 0874835615
$12.95
Ages 4-8

If you're traveling around the globe, these are great stories to share with your child about the legends and folklore from places around the world.

The Kids' Book of the 50 Great States: A State-by-State Scrapbook Filled with Facts, Maps, Puzzles, Poems, Photos, and More
Scholastic Trade
ISBN 0590996215
$14.95
Ages 6 and up
Gather ideas for items to bring back to your child based on what's listed in this scrapbook on the U.S. states. There's room for photos you take on your trip and for all sorts of memories and souvenirs.

The Scrambled States of America
by Laurie Keller
Henry Holt & Company
ISBN 0805058028
$16.95
The states of the U.S. get all mixed up in this fun children's story. All of the states are brightly colored shapes for younger readers to learn when you read together.

World Almanac for Kids 2000
Edited by Elaine Israel and World Almanac
St. Martin's Press
ISBN 0886878403
$10.95
Ages 9-12
The ultimate almanac for kids, including regular information like flags, history, and facts, as well as a great updated list of Web sites for further learning. For elementary readers too.

P. 83 TRAVEL JOURNALS

All About Me: A Keepsake Journal for Kids
by Linda Kranz
Rising Moon
ISBN 0873586581
$12.95
Ages 9-12
For kids having a tough time getting started and thinking of things to write about, *All About Me* is filled with ideas and starters for the young writer.

Doing the Days: A Year's Worth of Creative Journaling, Drawing, Listening, Reading, Thinking, Arts & Crafts Activities for Children Ages 8-12
by Lorraine M. Dahlstrom
Free Spirit Publishing
ISBN 0915793628
$21.95
Ages 8-12
This book is one year's worth of journal ideas, with hundreds of activities linked to the calendar year.

P. 89 COOKING TOGETHER

Kids Cooking: A Very Slightly Messy Manual/With Plastic Measuring Spoons
Klutz Press
ISBN 0932592147
$13.95
All ages
Sixty-five kid-friendly recipes to round out any family meal, complete with a set of color-coded measuring spoons.

Honest Pretzels: And 64 Other Amazing Recipes for Cooks Ages 8 & Up
by Mollie Katzen
Tricycle Press
ISBN 1883672880
$19.95
Ages 8 and up
The great thing about cookbooks by Mollie Katzen is that children are the cooks and adults are chef's assistants. All the recipes are vegetarian, very healthy, and employ all sorts of cooking techniques and skills for kids to learn.

Pretend Soup and Other Real Recipes: A Cookbook for Preschoolers & Up
by Mollie Katzen
Tricycle Press
ISBN 1883672066
$16.95
Ages 4-8
A great cookbook for cooking with very young children, this book teaches kids math, science, and working together, all while making things like chocolate-banana shakes and preschool popovers. A classic.

P. 103 IT'S A GRAND NEW FLAG

Flags of the World: 96 Full-Color Pressure Sensitive Stickers
by A.G. Smith
Dover Publications
ISBN 0486298213
$4.95
Ages 4-8
What child doesn't love stickers? Not all the countries of the world are here, but it's a fun and inexpensive addition to any flag activities you have together.

The State Flags of Our Nation
Thomas Publications
ISBN 1577470214
$5.95
All ages
A great resource for the business traveler who visits the states of the U.S., with all kinds of information on the banners of the 50 states.

The World Encyclopedia of Flags: The Definitive Guide to International Flags, Banners, Standards, and Ensigns
By Alfred Znamierowski
Lorenz Books
ISBN 0754801675
$40.00
A little heavy on the historical detail for kids, but the best resource book on the flags of the world now available. Great for older children who'll design the family flag with a view toward history and heraldry.

The Flags of the World Web site, with 9,300 images and a variety of serious flag hobbyists maintaining the site.

ENCYCLOPEDIA CD-ROMS

DK Children's Encyclopedia with CD-ROM
DK Publishing
ISBN 0789454769
$69.95
Ages 9-12
A great comprehensive and kid-friendly CD-ROM that features a fact-finder section, maps, charts, and U.S. and world history. For ages 9 and up, but with a little help even younger kids could get around most of this CD.

PARENTING WEB SITES

There are thousands of sites that cater to every aspect of parenting. Here are a few that provide information to help with the trials and tribulations of being a business traveling parent:

www.en-parent.com
The official site for The Entrepreneurial Parent, a work-family resource designed for home office entrepreneurs. Even if you don't work out of a home office, you'll find the site filled with information and support from the "National Association of 'EPs'".

www.tnpc.com
The National Parenting Center (TNPC) site features articles and question-and-answer sessions with a variety of experts. Comprehensive information and an award-winning site.

www.parentsoup.com
The best shopping for parents is here, from books to other materials for families. An easy to navigate design, too.

References

WEB SITES

www.britannica.com
The official Web site of Encyclopaedia Britannica, with a wealth of information from a well-known name in encyclopedic circles. A bit dry for kids at times, but the hundreds of links help find the answer for any questions about geography and other subjects.

www.mhkids.com
McGraw Hill Publishing Company's site for their kids' encyclopedias-this is a colorful, easy-to-use site that contains tons of information on the peoples and places of the world.

ALPHABET BOOKS

Alphabatics
by Suse MacDonald
Aladdin Paperbacks
ISBN 0689716257
$6.95
Ages 4-8
Each letter in this creative book becomes the word it represents, with the hole in b becoming a balloon and more. A Caldecott Honor winner.

Alphabet Antics: Hundreds of Activities to Challenge and Enrich Letter Learners of All Ages
by Ken Vinton. Edited by Pamela Espeland
Free Spirit Publishing
ISBN 1575420082
$19.95

For young learners writing their first letters, sending their first e-mails, or reading letters and faxes from Mom or Dad, this book is filled with activities for further family literacy activities.

Alphabet City
by Stephen T. Johnson
Viking Children's Books
ISBN 0670856312
$15.99
Ages 4-8
Although for younger readers, this book is twenty-six trick pictures that can stump even older readers who are trying to find the letters in the artwork. An award winner that will inspire family artists to hide their own letters in paintings and drawings.

The Graphic Alphabet
by David Pelletier
Orchard Books
ISBN 0531360016
$17.95
Ages 4-8
This clever Caldecott Honor book explores letters for what they are-beautiful and interesting shapes in themselves. You'll be inspired to create your child's letterhead together using his or her initials-some of the first letters he or she will probably learn-when you see the illustrations in this book.